SCHIRMER'S LIBRARY
OF MUSICAL CLASSICS

Vol. 1600

JOHANNES BRAHMS

Fifty-One Exercises

For the Piano

⊕

G. SCHIRMER, Inc.

DISTRIBUTED BY

HAL•LEONARD®
CORPORATION

7777 W. BLUEMOUND RD. P.O. BOX 13819 MILWAUKEE, WI 53213

Printed in the U. S. A.

51 Exercises

For the Piano

Johannes Brahms

1 a *)

*) **These and similar exercises should also be practised in other keys — for example, No. 1b in A major, No. 1c in E major, etc.
Variations in tempo and dynamics are left to the player's discretion.**

39476

1 b

1 c

1 d

1 e

1 f

2 a

2 b

*) To be continued into further octaves *ad lib.*

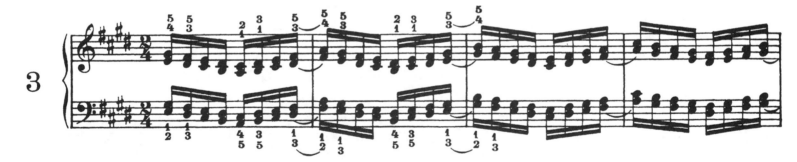

*) To be continued into further octaves *ad lib.*

*) Preparatory exercise for scales in sixths, in which (as with scales in thirds) the upper tones are connected in the ascent, and the lower tones in the descent.

*) Brief repetitions within an exercise (:|:) are *ad lib*.

**) Preparatory exercise for No. b

*) Preparatory exercise for No. 6

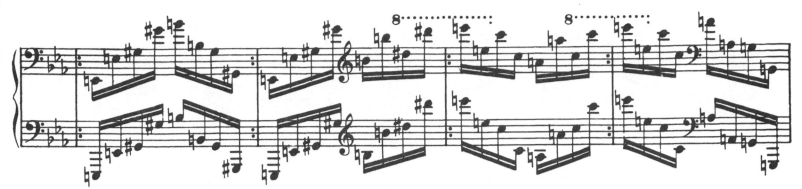

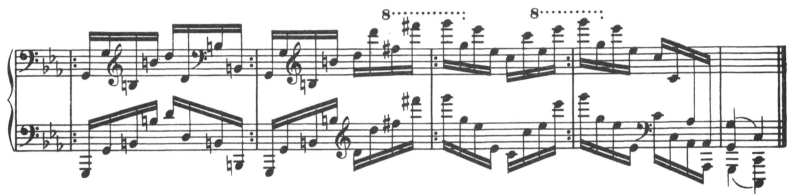

7

*) **Repetitions** (:‖:) are to be played in different octaves (one and two higher or lower) than written.

* Whole notes in parentheses (○) are not to be struck, but are to be depressed silently and held down throughout the exercise.

16 a

16 b

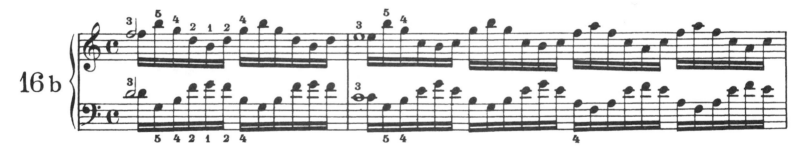

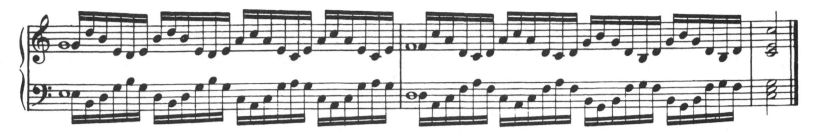

16c

17

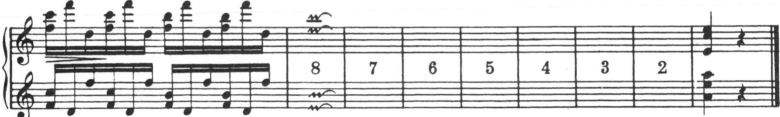

23 b

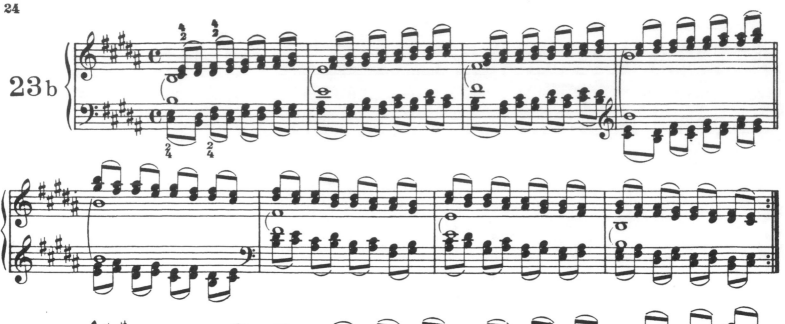

23 c

24 a *ben legato*

24b

Non troppo allegro

25a

25b

25c

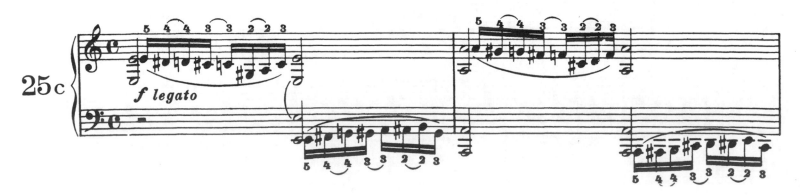

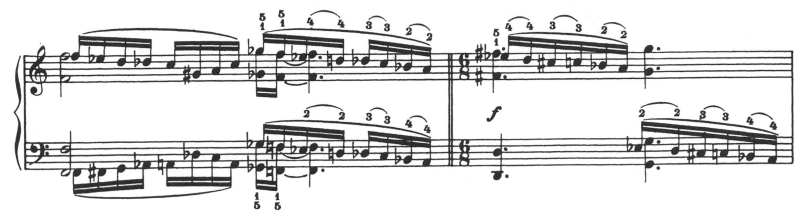

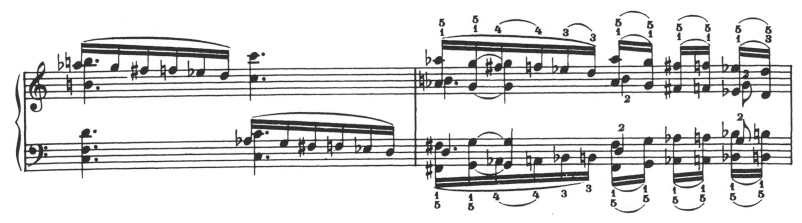

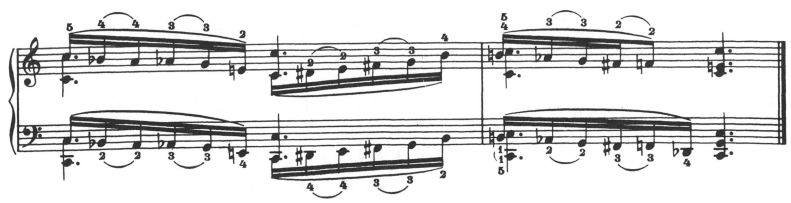

26c

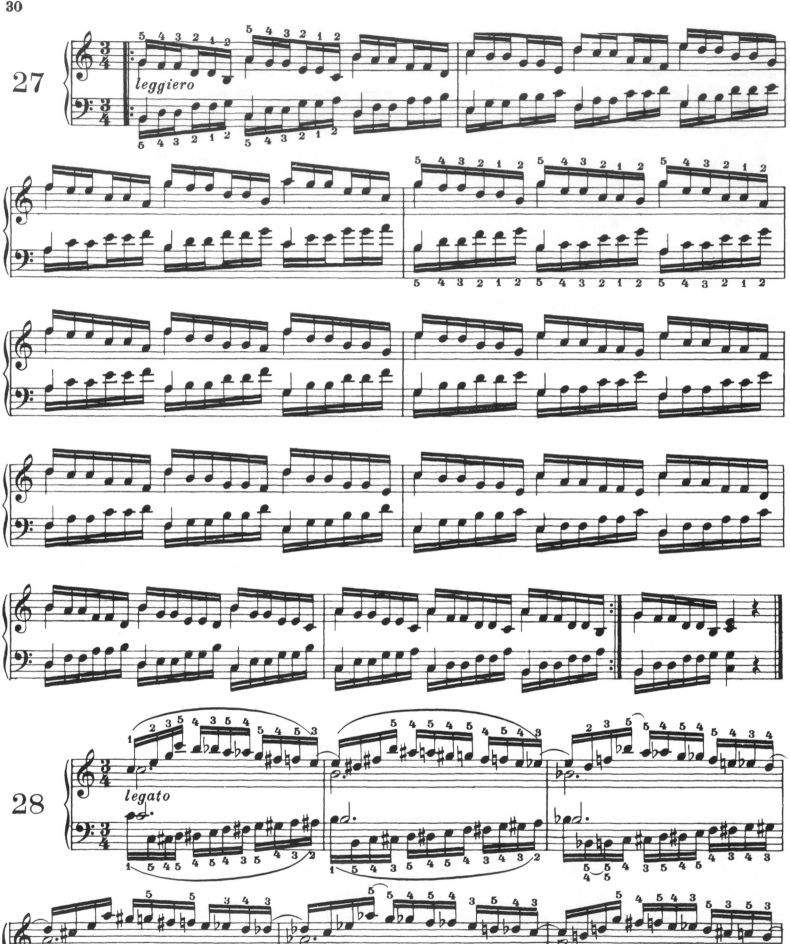

29

30

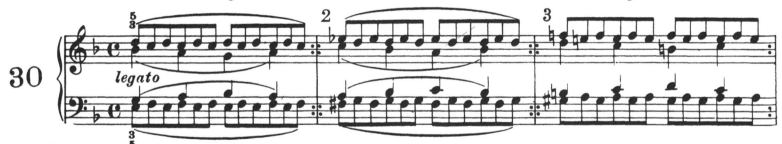

Non troppo Allegro

31a

31b

etc.

etc.

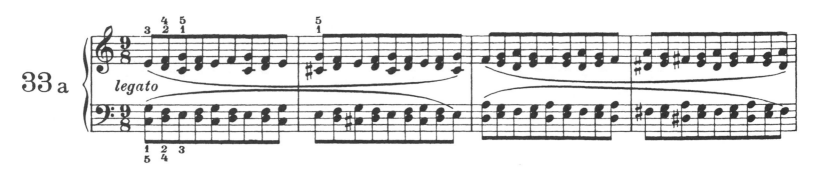

33 a

etc. come sopra.

33 b

legato

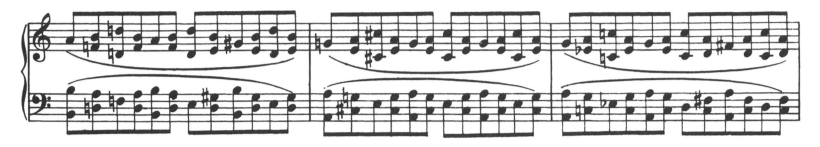

etc. come sopra

ben legato

34a

35

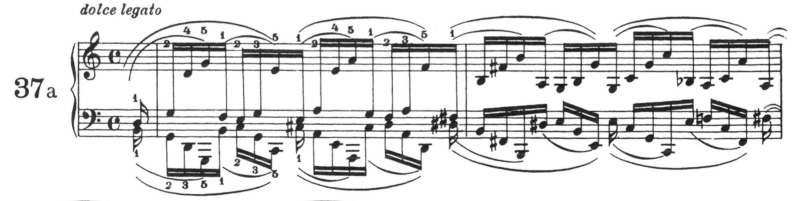

ben legato

39

40 a

etc. ad lib.

44

40b *leggiero o ben legato*

simile ad lib.

etc. ad lib.

41a simile ad lib.

41b

42 a

etc. ad lib.

42 b

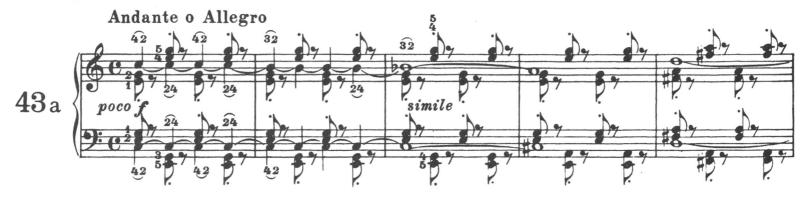

Andante o Allegro

43a

poco f

simile

Andante

43 b

etc. ad lib.

44 a

ben legato (o leggiero)

44 b

45

ben marcato

etc. simile come sopra

49 b

50

ben legato

ben legato

etc.
simile
ad lib.

51

Vivace

leggiero

(cresc.)

(dim.)